Liberation of the Mind

Collected Poems

Saoirse Ó Glasáin

Liberation of the Mind

Copyright © 2022 Saoirse Ó Glasáin

Cover artwork and illustrations by Saoirse Ó Glasáin

All rights reserved.

No part of this book may be reproduced or used in any manner without the prior written permission of the Poet/Artist, except for the use of brief quotations in a book review.

This work is intended for a mature audience.

ISBN: 9798814541208

For business enquiries please contact :
celtacosmoscreations@yahoo.com

@thepoetcouple

Other work from Celta Cosmos Creations :
Beyond Her Ninth Wave - Collected Poems by Jack Ó Glasáin

Mater

September Evening by a Stream

The Language of Nature

Society-a-Sunder

Provoking folks

Warrior of the Blue Flame

Alien

Free Will

Words - & - Rhymes

Seal of Amenti

Love Dance

Blood Reigns Royal

Liberation

Divine Feminine

Cernunnos

'Jack-the-Lad'

ATLANTIAN

Unknown

Dedication

I dedicate my art and words to the other half of my soul. Jack, you have been the catalyst for the direction of my life. You encourage me to always strive to be my best self. You are my inspiration, my motivation, my warrior, my protector, my divine masculine counterpart, my husband, my twin flame, the father to our children, a true leader and brother to mankind. Thank You for always having my back, supporting me in all of my endeavours – creative or otherwise. You push me to jump, to be who I was born to be. I love you.

Thank you for your patience and commitment. You are my guiding light.

Mater

The finest touch

Caressing bones,

Information a clutch

Silly student loans,

Not understanding much

Hearing nothing but moans,

Is that Spirit calling?

Lost in the noise

Of that silent chatter,

Seeing only solitude surrounded

By this seemingly solid Mater.

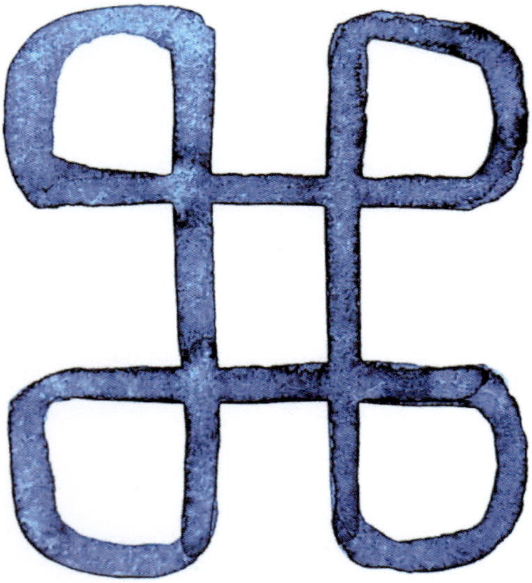

September Evening by a Stream

Ripe air, cow trodden road,
A trickle of a stream,
Rain drops dancing in the wind,
Layers of green as far as the eye can see.

Swallows swooping, twittering away,
Multiple different tones of grey,
The neighbours wave in-passing,
This day is nothing but a blessing.

Soggy moss on a concrete wall,
Red berries, nettles, Hawthorne too,
Farmers working, fertilizing fields,
A little chill; but the warmth of my husband is near.

The Language of Nature

Silvery flickers of light

Dipping ducks

Hints of firey gold and red

The world seems to stand still here

Looking out on this view.

Cawing crow, watching from above

A glimpse of the void in this Great Unknown

Gifts of grace

From the veiled mystery

A soul released through the heart

All it took was peace.

Society-a-Sunder

Pollination; inflation

Pineal gland activation

In a pile of denial

Inversion; deflection

In a state of disgrace

Tutting... a tiresome trait

Criticism and commentary

A glossy gossipy glow

Society-a-sunder

Is it any wonder?

Provoking Folks

Provoking folks and

Laughing at jokes

21st century hoax.

Wannabe heroes

Drinkin' 7up zeros

We're all just a

Bunch of weirdos.

Warrior of the Blue Flame

Born for a purpose

Protector of her flame

Listening out for answers

Within the whispers that came

Leaving the body; other worldly perception

Seemingly shy;

Observing;

Retention.

Alien

Am I the only one like this?

Do others think like me?

Do they know I'm different

I can't tell if they don't see

Everything seems so alien

I'm safe here within my mind

A refuge from the chaotic crimes

And these so-called end of times.

Free Will

Plunging into the watery depths of the heart
Searching for our start in order to depart
From this three-dimensional plane to the next domain
Wondering.. wishing.. wanting..
For those ever-moving goal posts to just stop.
HA! The spiral never stops.
Light, dark, light, dark,
On the cusp of that beautifully balanced fulcrum
Patiently waiting to see what we will become.
A powerfully paradoxical play out of events,
Building tangible tension
Piercing the invisible walls of phantom self; remaining still
Trust promising a golden path for our.. Free Will.

Words - & - Rhymes

My mind; filled with lines

Of endless words and rhymes

Trying to declutter so I can reutter

The golden threads of thoughts sublime.

Thinking of the greats; W.B Yeats,

A.E Russell and Blake

No one can forsake the words these men remake

Retold through the resilient and strong

Strength of soul, heart and wrongs

Frantically forgiving all facets of being

Becoming free to be, authentically me.

Seal of Amenti

Halls of Amenti
Hidden in the heart
Pearly gates of heaven
Mystery school an art
Defining determination
Overcoming fractured parts.

Love Dance

Ground, Snake,

Creative, centred,

Tube lit, trance bit

Sweet, salty, hard to resist.

Heart to tongue

Energy flowing strong,

Inch by inch, heart filling up.

Building the divine,

One channel at a time,

Closer to home each day that passes.

Keep on fighting,

You'll see what will be,

A destiny fulfilled,

And a wife; that's me.

Blood Reigns Royal

Keeping the lion tamed
Royal blood reigns.
Reaching for the heights
Loyal men unite
Protecting Danu's light
Never giving up the fight
Unleasing that inner animal
Gaining something insightful
Detachment from emotional ties
Royal blood reigns.

Liberation

Whiskey, vodka, gin,

Discovering the origin

Of the human race

Accelerated pace

Coming to conclusions

Amidst all the confusion

Of the non-sensical noise

Created without poise.

Feeling like you're in a trap

Not wanting to ever look back

Invisible prison walls

Realization: The illusion

Is at our beck and call

Projected perception

No power without participation

Why thank you sir, for our liberation.

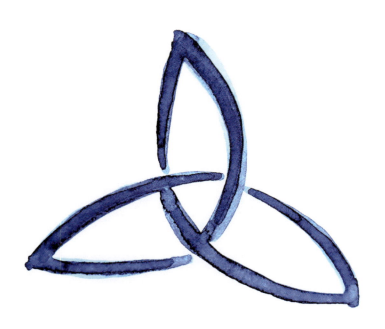

Divine Feminine

This land has been

Taken for granted

Everyone has raved and ranted

Have the people ever even seen

Soil like this, more supreme

No wonder why

It's been raped and disgraced

Again and again

This magic island refills

Rich pastures and trees

Lakelands and bees.

Rejuvenating, replenishing

Men falling on their knees

To worship the Green Goddess

Her mysterious majesty interwoven

Through threads of time.

The feminine divine.

Cernunnos

A muse for men
Friend to La Femme
Vitality for the virgin
Defender of devotion
Seduced by sirens
Asfixiation; dilation
Happily hypnotized
Witty Wittan Witch
Reaching deep within her well
The sorceress' spell
Cosmic Celtos Cave
Glimmering glittery wave
Elusive; erotic; enchantress.

'Jack-the-Lad'

Green growth

Oak king; Christ sings

Life-force; lover

Trickster; reviver; brother

Aggression; altered perception

Fertilizer of fates

Miraculous Moose relates.

ATLANTIAN

Murky, misty mind

Unfurling... one-of-a-kind

Tenous transformation

Remembering a forgotten nation

North-eastern lands

Uncovering the Universe's plans

Clarifying thoughts of inspiration

Rectifying all karma; non-negotiation

Wandering around the land of Fae

Tip-toeing gently; no dismay

Swallowing pride; losing control

Willingly surrendering to play my roll

Total transparency, gathering fragments

Freeing Earth and her soul entrapments.

Unknown

Through the depths of consciousness,

We merge the mind, and loose the binds.

Speaking the words of men, sage smokin'

Spirit cleansed. The earth warrior bends.

Remaining 'separate', yet one.

Confined by the illusion of Time and Space,

Never really forgotten the true Celtos race.

Engrained into the DNA, ancient sacred language of fire,

Calling us home, through the Great Unknown.

...

Printed in Great Britain
by Amazon